SPACE JUNK:

POLLUTION BEYOND THE EARTH

Judy Donnelly and
Sydelle Kramer

MORROW JUNIOR BOOKS   New York

For Joy

ACKNOWLEDGMENTS

The authors wish to thank the following experts for the invaluable information and assistance which made this book possible: Donald Kessler, head of Orbital Debris Studies, Johnson Space Center; Paul Maley, Rockwell Shuttle Operations Company, Johnson Space Center; Herbert A. Zook, space scientist, Johnson Space Center; Captain Thomas Niemann, public affairs officer, United States Space Command, Cheyenne Mountain; and David L. Crawford, chairman of the American Astronomical Society's Environmental Pollution Committee.

We are especially grateful to Marc Feldman, senior scientist in engineering, the University of Rochester; Nicholas L. Johnson, author of *Artificial Space Debris* (Orbit Book Company) and advisory scientist, Teledyne Brown Engineering; and Jonathan Platt, astronomer, American Museum of Natural History–Hayden Planetarium for reading the manuscript; and to our editor, Andrea Curley, for her guidance and support.

Printed in the United States of America.   1 2 3 4 5 6 7 8 9 10

Library of Congress Cataloging-in-Publication Data Donnelly, Judy. Space junk : pollution beyond the earth / Judy Donnelly and Sydelle Kramer. p.   cm. Includes index. Summary: Discusses the miscellaneous junk floating in space, how it got there, what effects it can have, and what can be done about it. ISBN 0-688-08678-0. —ISBN 0-688-08679-9 (lib. bdg.) 1. Space debris—Juvenile literature.   [1. Space debris.] I. Kramer, Sydelle.   II. Title. TL1489.D66 1990 363.73'0919—dc20   89-13544   CIP   AC

PHOTO CREDITS

Permission for the following photographs is gratefully acknowledged: Courtesy Department Library Services, American Museum of Natural History, pp. 9 (neg. no. 2A4127), 11 (neg. no. 299663), 13 (neg. no. 2A6849), 15 (neg. no. 118314); Teledyne Brown Engineering, pp. 3, 53; U.S. Air Force, Peterson Air Force Base, Colorado, pp. 63, 78; U.S. Space Command, Cheyenne Mountain, Colorado, pp. 76, 77; Yale University Library (photograph courtesy Department Library Services, American Museum of Natural History, neg. no. 327061, photo: Schulze), p. 21. All other photographs courtesy of NASA.

Contents

Introduction

Time: the present.

Place: a few hundred miles above Earth.

You're traveling through space. All around you is a black sky that never grows light. In the distance you see the moon, the sun, and the stars. Beneath you, Earth is softly glowing, spinning silently in a blue-green haze.

But suddenly a flash of light dazzles you. It's getting brighter and brighter—it's hurtling right toward you. You and your fellow astronauts watch it approach, unable to move. What could it be? An alien spaceship? An enemy missile? A falling star?

The light streaks closer and closer. Now you're really getting worried. In the cabin of your spacecraft you all hold your breath. Then someone hits a button on the instrument panel, and on the screen in front of you, you suddenly see what the light is. You and the other astronauts start laughing. It's only a screwdriver, lost in space—just another piece of space junk, like the ones you've seen before.

Funny? Yes. Science fiction fantasy? Not really. All kinds of man-made clutter are circling the planet Earth right now—we even know a screwdriver was once in orbit. And although astronauts today can't actually identify each hunk of trash the way they do in this imaginary scene, space junk is a real danger to them and to the world's space programs.

How did it all get up there? Why didn't anybody stop it?

When burned-out rocket stages kept circling Earth, or satellites stopped working but didn't fall from the sky, nobody worried too much about it. After all, people told themselves, space stretched on and on, like an empty ocean that never reaches a shore. When flecks of paint peeled off spacecraft or when astronauts on spacewalks dropped some of their tools, nobody thought it would be a problem.

But even though space seems to go on forever, we depend on the part of it that is closest to the surface of the Earth. In the same way our air and water have

Every dot in this computer-produced picture stands for an object orbiting Earth. About 95 percent is space junk.

grown dirty over the years, this fraction of space closest to our planet is slowly filling up with junk. Today there are millions of pieces of debris above us, from bits tinier than a thumbtack to rockets as tall as a three-story house. And every piece, even a small one, can damage a spacecraft and put the lives of astronauts in danger.

More and more garbage is created every day. Sometimes old and useless spacecraft tumble back to Earth.

If one landed on a city, lives could be threatened. Sometimes rocket stages that have been traveling near the surface of the Earth for years will explode. Chunks of metal then spread out hundreds of miles across our sky. Sometimes one piece of space junk crashes into another. More garbage is created and ends up traveling around the Earth. Sometimes bits of debris collide with spacecraft carrying people. On one space shuttle mission a window was damaged.

So far we've been lucky. No terrible space junk accident has occurred. But some experts feel our luck may soon run out. An American space station might be launched before the end of this century—will it ram into a hunk of junk and explode into smithereens? The United States is also sending a huge telescope beyond Earth—will it smack into a blob of garbage and never work right again? Special weapons that are powered by nuclear energy are being built for space—will one of them smash into floating metal and rain radiation on our planet? Satellites are orbiting above us—will one crash in flames to the ground, setting fires and injuring people?

How will we get rid of all this garbage? Can scientists change the world's space program so less litter gets left behind? What are experts doing to protect spacecraft from space junk? Can we even locate all the dangerous debris up in the sky? So much of it is swimming around us that astronomers fear they might mistake bits of it for distant new stars!

In the next few years there will be even more trash.

It can threaten the lives of those who soar into space. One day the biggest pieces may threaten those who stay behind on the ground.

If we want to stay free to explore the universe, space junk is a problem we are going to have to solve. After all, there's no space sanitation team to come to the rescue. Does this mean the garbage above us will haunt Earth forever? What are we doing to stop the pollution? Can space ever be the same now that earthlings have reached it? The future of space exploration may depend on how we answer these questions. This book may help *you* figure out some of the answers.

A Dream of Space

It took billions of years for the sky curved above us, for the blackness beyond it stretching farther than we can imagine, to become the way they are today. We here on our planet had to study space for centuries before we could understand much about it.

Our universe is older than the dinosaurs, older than the planet Earth itself. It may have begun in what is called the Big Bang. About 17 billion years ago, scientists believe, there was a colossal explosion—nuclear fireworks. Afterward gas formed. It was extremely hot—perhaps as sizzling as 10 million degrees Fahrenheit. Because the gas was so hot, it expanded and expanded, like bubbles that grow and grow but never burst. The universe simply got larger and larger.

Then, slowly, the gas cooled off. Huge clouds formed, made of gas and dust. As the clouds got even cooler, the dust gathered into chunks. The chunks grew harder and thicker and bigger and bigger. Over billions of years they joined up with one another. Finally, they formed galaxies. One was our own, the Milky Way. Afterward came our solar system, with the sun and all the planets. The Earth is 4.5 billion years old.

But not all this first gas and dust got used up in making the galaxies. A lot of it is still out there somewhere among the stars. Some of it is jammed together to make comets and meteors and asteroids. And some of it is invisible—scientists call it dark matter.

The first people on Earth didn't know what the universe was made of. In the eastern part of Africa, they were born and grew up 1.75 million years ago. That's a long time to us but less than a minute to the universe. What did these ancient people think of outer space? Even before they had a word for it, they felt something mysterious stretched above them. Just as we do today, they gazed up at the sky. Just as we do today, they wondered what surrounded them. They knew the sun warmed their bodies and the moon lit up the night. They knew the stars blinked at them from a place they'd never been.

Animals played a large part in the way the ancient Hindus saw the sky.

Still, on a night 1.75 million years ago, the sky didn't look quite the same as it does now. The stars shone down then from different places. It took almost 1.9 million years for the sky to look exactly like it does now. And as the centuries pass, the stars' positions keep changing. The grandchildren of your grandchildren's grandchildren may not see quite the same night sky we do.

But no matter where the stars are or which ones we are looking at, whether we were born thousands of years ago or just yesterday, there's something about space that's mysterious and exciting. Humankind's very first dream may have been about the stars.

Our ancestors couldn't travel to space, but they might have felt closer to it than we do. All that they could see seemed somehow to belong to them. They didn't know, as we do, that the stars are so far away from Earth. When they stepped outside and looked around, space just seemed like the roof of their world. They had no telescopes, but they believed they viewed the sky clearly. They had no instruments, but they were sure they knew how powerful the sun was. No machine had been invented yet to tell them about the universe. They had only their senses to teach them what they wanted to learn.

As time went by, early people began to study the stars. At first they thought space was flat and stretched no farther than they could see. They thought the moon was shaped like a plate and was as smooth as their skin. Each group had different ideas about what they saw. The Egyptians were sure what was above us was a tent top. Another group called the Sumerians believed the stars ended up in a river. When the stars disappeared from the sky at dawn, they swam for a long time through waters wide and deep. When they finally reached the shore, the stars climbed back into the sky.

Ancient people were certain the heavens weren't empty. Somewhere, they thought, beyond where they could see, were the palaces of their gods, dazzling in their beauty. From their thrones, those who ruled the universe could look down on Earth and watch how everyone lived.

As the centuries passed, our ancestors began to realize

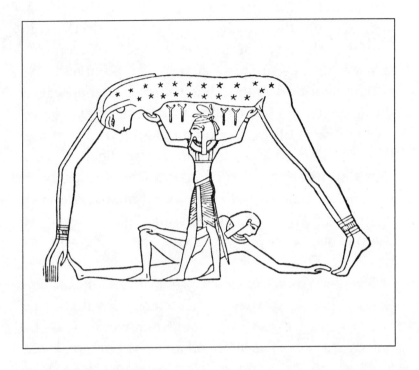

The early Egyptians believed the sky was held up by one of their gods.

how complicated space was. The sky still seemed nearby, but it was full of mystery. The moon changed its shape, the stars slowly moved across the heavens. The sun rose and set from different places along the horizon. The shadows it made grew longer, then shorter. Finally people understood that they could tell time by watching the sky.

Was winter due to arrive? The stars told the answer. When was the longest day of the year? The sun revealed the secret. From the changing face above them, they learned about the seasons. Farmers gazed overhead to see if they should plant their vegetables. They were able to read the sky's message about when to harvest.

Then about seven thousand years ago, people called the Babylonians invented the first calendar. It was based on the phases of the moon and wasn't very accurate. But only five hundred years later, the Egyptians, by watching the stars carefully, developed a calendar of 365 days. Another two thousand years passed. The Egyptians, Babylonians, Indians, and Chinese began the study of astronomy by observing the changes in the heavens.

Seventeen more centuries went by before the ancient Greeks developed what we call science. Science is one of the ways we can understand our world. It is the orderly study of facts about all aspects of nature, based on observing, investigating, and experimenting.

The Greeks assumed that the world was logical, that they could figure it out. They were the first to realize they could use mathematical formulas to explain what they couldn't see. These formulas led them to develop theories, or hunches, that explain why things happen. They made these new ideas part of science, too.

The Greeks also named some of the stars. They, and the Romans after them, thought they saw patterns in the sky. The stars appeared to group themselves into familiar figures. When they looked on the night, they recognized part of their world above them. They saw animals, everyday objects, even heroes who had once lived on Earth. There were a dog and a bear, a lion and a dolphin, an archer and a soldier.

These groups of stars are called constellations. The first sailors used them as guides when they explored the seas. The sky was a huge map that showed them where their home was. By following the constellations, they taught themselves navigation—how to travel across the oceans.

Up to five hundred years ago, people believed Earth was the center of the universe. Didn't everything in the sky seem to move around our planet? It wasn't until 1543, nearly a lifetime after Columbus, that scientists began to understand how the Solar System works. That

For thousands of years, people struggled to understand the workings of the universe, as this woodcut from the Middle Ages suggests.

year a Pole named Nicolaus Copernicus realized the Earth traveled around the sun. So, he figured out, did all the other planets. They were following paths that we now know as orbits.

When an object in space flies around another, larger object, the path it follows is called an orbit. All the planets, including Earth, orbit the sun. They speed along silently in the same direction. The moon, smaller than our planet, orbits Earth. When a space shuttle shoots around the globe, it's orbiting Earth, too.

At first scientists like Copernicus thought orbits were perfect circles. But in 1609 a German named Johannes Kepler discovered that they weren't. A planet's orbit is elliptical, or oval.

That same year an Italian named Galileo Galilei built the first powerful telescope. When he pointed it at the sky he could see the moon had craters. He spotted the four largest of Jupiter's moons. Everything he saw convinced him Copernicus was right.

Now scientists were moving closer to understanding the universe. But they still didn't know how human beings could explore space. Many believed that it would never happen. Yet today rockets often shoot toward the stars. The world has changed, along with our knowledge of it. People ask different questions; they try to

Seventeenth-century astronomers used a device called a quadrant for observing the stars.

Fig. K.

solve different problems. There are brilliant scientists who study nothing but what's above us. There are inventors who build instruments that help explain the Solar System. People still stare at the stars and wonder at their beauty, but now they dare to fly out toward them, not just watch them from the ground.

Now it's possible that one day space will be just another place to visit, a not-too-distant neighborhood where some of our friends will be moving. Our dreams today are very different from the dreams of those who came before us. We imagine soaring through the heavens like we skateboard down city blocks. We have visions of finding life in galaxies as beautiful as ours. Many of us feel that space is where the future lies, and we have plans to make it our own.

The frontier above our heads just might solve some of Earth's problems. Certain products that we need are slightly flawed when they're made on the ground, but in space, away from Earth's gravity, they can be produced perfectly. Lenses for cameras and microscopes, computer chips and crystals, even some very important types of drugs will all be made in orbiting laboratories. In the twenty-first century, when you've become a grandparent, it's possible our supply of some minerals will run out. Then we might turn to the moon for them. Or rockets could tow asteroids close to our planet so that the minerals buried in them can be mined for our use.

Someday the world may be so crowded with people that part of the population will have to move away. A nuclear war or some other disaster might occur, and everyone here on Earth will have to flee. But some experts believe we don't have to worry. There'll be new places to live, new lands on which to build. Space will provide us with everything we need. There'll be sparkling new cities rising on other planets. There'll be young pioneers beginning new colonies. All our electricity will come from the sun's power. We'll even take vacations in fancy hotels among the stars.

But will all these dreams have a chance to come true? Or does space junk, as some scientists believe, threaten our plans for the future?

2

The Drawing Board

Today more than a hundred rockets blast off each year, and almost everyone on Earth knows we can travel in space. Before you were born, men walked on the moon and astronauts lived in a space station two hundred fifty miles high. The machines that went toward the stars were the most complicated ever invented, taller than apartment buildings and jammed with millions of parts. But from the instant the first rocket stayed up

instead of coming down, our planet had a new problem
—space junk.

How did it get up there in the first place?

Rockets, of course, were the beginning. In the 1200s,
the Chinese invented them as weapons of war. Their
historians called them "arrows of flying fire." But these
rockets were very small and no one really knew exactly
where they would land. Then, many years later, a man
named William Congreve made them bigger and more
powerful. It was during the War of 1812, and the English were fighting the Americans. Suddenly one night
the English fired rockets at Baltimore, Maryland. As the
rockets exploded and burned like falling stars, Francis
Scott Key wrote about their red glare. Americans heard
all about rockets from "The Star-Spangled Banner."

Almost fifty years later a Frenchman named Jules
Verne realized that rockets could be used for something
more than war. In his book *From the Earth to the Moon*,
he wrote about men flying through space using rockets.
People all over the world read his book. One of them
was a Russian schoolteacher named Konstantin Tsiolkovsky.

Tsiolkovsky believed in Verne's dream of space travel,
of rockets soaring through the universe like giant eagles
without wings. He was the first one to understand how
to build and shape a rocket—in parts called stages
which, put together, looked like a bullet. He figured
out the most powerful fuel a rocket could use to pull
away from the Earth's gravity and sail through airless
space.

This illustration from Jules Verne's *From the Earth to the Moon* shows a nineteenth-century version of a rocket train in space.

It wasn't until 1926, however, that some of Tsiol-kovsky's ideas were tested. That year an American teacher named Robert Goddard did something no one had done before: He built a test rocket, a very small version of the sort he thought could blast into space. Just ten feet high and no wider than your leg, Goddard's rocket couldn't travel even the length of a city block. But because it took off and flew, Goddard knew his ideas would work.

No one built a rocket that could enter space until the early 1940s. During World War II, Nazi scientists built rockets over five stories high that could travel as fast as thirty-five hundred miles per hour. These rockets, called V-2s, were the first to fly up where there was no oxygen. The Nazis filled them with bombs and shot them toward England. The rockets cut through the clouds in silence so no one could hear them coming. They charged down to Earth and no one knew how to stop them.

When the war ended, some of the Nazi rocket scientists came to America. Others became citizens of the Soviet Union. With their knowledge they helped both countries build gigantic rockets—rockets that could take us up into space. Some people felt that whoever made the best ones could rule the skies. And if a country could do that, it would be the most powerful in the world.

But many other people believed space should have nothing to do with war. To them, the heavens belonged to everyone. What one country achieved should be on behalf of the whole world.

Robert Goddard with the rocket he test-launched in 1926. People once ridiculed him for his ideas; today he is considered the father of modern rocketry.

Scientists and engineers began to devote their studies to space travel and rockets. But despite the work of Tsiolkovsky and Goddard, there were many unanswered questions about how to roam beyond the clouds. How exactly would the best rockets work? Were Tsiolkovsky and Goddard right about what the most powerful fuel would be? Would a rocket be able to return a person safely to Earth?

Experts knew that in order to reach space a rocket had to travel fast enough to escape the pull of gravity. It is gravity that gives everything here on Earth its weight. As if our planet had long fingers, it draws us down and makes sure we don't sail off into the clouds. Its grip is so strong that in order to go into orbit, a rocket must travel very fast—nearly five miles per second. You can barely take one step forward in a second, yet a rocket can zoom five miles in that time!

To go that fast a rocket must have powerful fuel. But which fuel should be used? Some were liquid and some were solid. Scientists decided to follow Tsiolkovsky's and Goddard's advice. They would use liquid fuel—a liquid made from hydrogen. But liquid fuel doesn't contain any oxygen. Since no fuel will burn without oxygen, and no oxygen exists above Earth's atmosphere, how can a rocket keep burning its liquid fuel once it gets into airless space?

Engineers followed Tsiolkovsky's and Goddard's designs. They built a rocket that carries its own oxygen. The oxygen is stored on board as a liquid. The fuel and the oxygen flow out of separate tanks and mix in what is called the combustion chamber. The combustion chamber is made of such strong material that it doesn't melt even though the fuel is burning. Fuel that's burning produces gases that get very hot. When gases are that hot, they stretch and expand. The combustion chamber fills up completely; and when there's no more room, the gases try to escape. At the bottom of the rocket are holes called nozzles. The gases push through the nozzles and gush out like steam. All this happens in a matter of seconds. Then the rocket thunders upward in the direction opposite to the gases. This forward motion of the rocket is what scientists have named thrust. The more gas escapes, the greater the rocket's thrust. The greater the thrust, the faster the rocket goes.

A rocket can have thrust even in space. That's because rockets don't take off by pushing against the ground. They take off because of what a scientist named Isaac Newton called the third law of motion. Three hundred years ago Newton discovered that every action has an equal and opposite reaction. When a rocket is launched, its gases shoot in one direction (the action) while it blasts off in the other (the reaction). If a rocket fires its engines in space, they spew gases in one direction, moving the rocket the opposite way.

To send a rocket a long distance—to the moon or to other planets—a huge amount of thrust is needed. In order to get out of Earth orbit and head toward the moon, a rocket must travel at twenty-five thousand miles per hour.

But it won't have enough thrust unless it has more

A three-stage *Apollo-Saturn V* rocket on the launching pad. The first and second stages will burn up and fall back to Earth; the third stage always becomes space junk.

than one section, or stage, to keep it speeding ahead. The stages fire one at a time, each building on the speed of the last to push the rocket ahead faster and faster. Every stage has its own engines and fuel—perhaps five engines in each stage burning three thousand gallons a second. That's like using up three swimming pools of fuel every minute! The stage drops off the rocket, or is jettisoned, when it runs out of fuel. A rocket with more than one stage is called a multistage rocket. It might be thirty stories high with each stage piled on the others like blocks.

Rockets got us past the clouds, but it was the stages they left behind that were the first pieces of space junk. In the first few years, no one worried about these jettisoned hulks. Scientists knew stages orbiting very close to our planet, many no more than one hundred miles high, would be pulled back to Earth by the tug of gravity. Then some would tumble into the ocean; others would burn to a crisp in Earth's atmosphere.

Anything falling to Earth from space has to pass through the atmosphere. The atmosphere consists of gases and tiny bits, called particles, of dust, and it completely surrounds our planet. Whatever is falling toward Earth, no matter how large or small, is moving so quickly you can't see what it is. It might be speeding toward you at up to twenty-five thousand miles per hour, so all your eyes pick up is a flash of light. As it enters the atmosphere it scrapes through the gases and rubs up against the particles. This scraping and rubbing is known as friction. Friction makes the object so hot it begins to burn; the object gets so hot its temperature might reach fifty-two hundred degrees Fahrenheit. If Earth got that hot, almost everything on it would burn up in an instant.

When a rocket stage falls through the atmosphere, it bursts into flames and crumbles into pieces. But if this always happens, how do American astronauts and Soviet cosmonauts return to Earth safely? Spacecraft that carry people are made of very special materials. These materials, which include metals like titanium and beryllium, protect the rocket when it enters the atmosphere so it doesn't melt or burn up.

When time passed and more and more multistage rockets shot into space, scientists slowly realized they were going to be a problem. Not all the rocket stages that were jettisoned fell into the ocean; not all of them were trapped in the atmosphere and caught fire. Some jettisoned rocket stages didn't come back at all. They weren't close enough to Earth to be pulled down quickly by gravity, so they settled into orbits high above us. They had entered space traveling at breathtaking speeds, and they didn't need to fire their engines to keep speeding along. There wasn't anything up there to slow them down and let gravity get hold of them— no dust, no gas, no air. Instead there was a force that was actually keeping them up—the same kind of force that affects all space junk.

You know gravity tries to pull down whatever is near Earth. But something else can balance gravity out— centrifugal force. Centrifugal force occurs when any

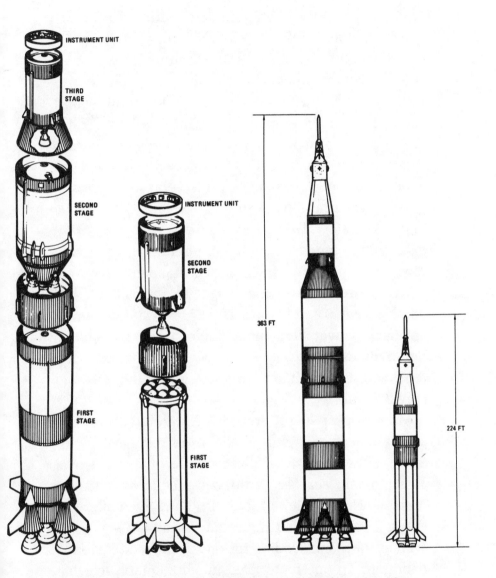

INSTRUMENT UNIT

THIRD
STAGE

SECOND
STAGE

INSTRUMENT UNIT

SECOND
STAGE

FIRST
STAGE

FIRST
STAGE

363 FT

224 FT

This diagram shows two multistage rockets: the three-stage *Saturn V (left)* and the two-stage *Saturn IB (right)*. Every time a rocket stage separates, various parts—clamps, bolts, springs, panels—fly into space to become space junk.

object, large or small, whips in a circle around any other object. As long as the object is moving at high speed, centrifugal force shoves it away from Earth.

So gravity breathes you in at the same time centrifugal force breathes you out. As the two pull against each other, an object's path curves into an orbit. Unless that object is a rocket that can fire its engines to keep it racing along, eventually it will slow down. If it's just a dead rocket stage—or any piece of space junk—gravity will triumph, centrifugal force will fade. The object will slowly sink toward Earth. No one knows exactly how long that can take. Scientists are sure the lower the orbit, the faster it will happen. There are objects close to Earth that might be in space for just another year. Then the atmosphere will slow them up and gravity will drag them down. But other objects hundreds of miles above us may orbit for centuries, moving fast enough and staying high enough to avoid gravity's pull.

Many rocket stages are now whizzing around our planet. They're zipping along on all kinds of paths. Some paths are as round as a circle, some are as oval as a football; some go around the equator, some go from the North Pole to the South Pole. Even after scientists discovered that many stages had become junk, even as they kept sending rockets up and adding to the pollution, no one really paid much attention to what was happening. Nothing could stop humanity from exploring the new frontier. That seemed more important than any litter overhead.

3

Blast-off

The history of the world changed on October 4, 1957. Up to that day, the only objects in space were natural ones that had been there for billions of years. But suddenly something new was orbiting Earth, something that hadn't been born along with the universe.

It was called *Sputnik I,* and the Soviet Union had launched it. It weighed 184 pounds and was about two feet across. Americans quickly nicknamed it the "flying basketball." Sitting firmly atop a rocket just like the point of a pencil, it shot into space and circled the Earth every ninety-five minutes.

Sputnik I was a satellite, the first one made by people. A satellite is an object that orbits another, larger object. The moon is Earth's satellite; Earth is the sun's satellite. There had been natural satellites like these almost from time's beginning. And now *Sputnik,* an artificial satellite, was up in space among the stars.

Americans were both excited and disappointed about *Sputnik I.* People had taken their first step into the universe—but the United States had wanted that step to be its own. Before America could send its own satellite up, the Soviets blasted yet another into space. It was November 3 when *Sputnik II* began circling the globe. On board was a dog named Laika. She was the first living thing from the Earth to travel to the heavens. But she never returned—the Soviets didn't know how to bring her back. She died painlessly in space from a poison mixed into her food.

Now when Americans stared at the sky, they thought of those Soviet Sputniks zooming overhead. There was nothing up in space that was American-made. While the United States vowed to catch up somehow, the Soviets fought hard to stay ahead. So the space race got started. Which nation would win? Which one would lift the first astronaut above the clouds? Which one would land the first person on the moon? Which one would be able to orbit Earth the longest?

This race has been going on now for over thirty years. It's a lot older than you, and it's older than some of your parents. But even when it first began, the United States and the Soviet Union agreed about something: The space race wasn't just about sending people higher and farther; it was also about learning all we could about the universe. Space could be our wisest teacher, revealing some of Earth's most hidden secrets. It was an empty frontier, with no borders or countries, so spacecraft could fly wherever they wanted. They might solve mysteries at the ends of the Milky Way or unravel riddles just above our heads. They would be our eyes and our ears, and they could discover anything.

Nobody in the United States thought much about space junk—after all, American scientists hadn't even gotten an object into orbit yet.

As the U.S. space program started up, the National Aeronautics and Space Administration made a decision. There would be three different ways America would conquer the heavens. The first was the one everyone knew about—flying astronauts past the clouds to roam through space. Some people didn't pay much attention to the others—putting satellites into orbit and launching unmanned rockets called probes. But scientists knew all three were important. Astronauts would tell us what space looked and felt like; they'd experience weightlessness and the fastest speeds anyone had ever traveled. Satellites would show us what was happening on Earth—predicting weather, uncovering pollution, watching over both land and sea. They would make communications better among all countries of the world. Probes would explore places people couldn't

In 1959, seven pilots became America's first astronauts.

reach, flying for years to the most distant planets and reporting back what they were like. Probes could land wherever scientists wanted them to—on dangerous surfaces where people might not survive.

For America the first step was to get a satellite into space. Scientists fired rocket after rocket, trying to find one that worked perfectly. Finally, less than a year after *Sputnik,* the United States launched its first satellite, *Explorer I.* It weighed only ten pounds, about as much as your leg; but it was jammed full of instruments, all of them miniatures.

Explorer I made a very important discovery. It found two strips of deadly radiation near Earth that were named the Van Allen belts. The radiation was stuck there as if it were held by a magnet. Could it slice though a rocket and kill the astronauts inside? Would it ruin all the instruments inside satellites and probes?

There was so much we humans didn't know about space! Suddenly scientists feared there might be other secret dangers. Would it turn out that space was too menacing to explore? We didn't want to send people where they could never be safe.

More rockets and satellites had to be launched. NASA began experiments to answer all kinds of questions. When rockets fired, they rattled and shook—could the vibrations injure astronauts? Blast-off would be noisy— would it make them all deaf? In space they'd be weight-less—would they be able to digest their food? There'd be no gravity—would that keep their hearts from pumping blood? Some scientists thought space might scramble the human brain. Others believed people would go crazy hundreds or thousands of miles from Earth.

It was hard to be sure of anything, but America had to try. So seven courageous men were chosen to be astronauts. The United States hoped one of them would be the first human in space.

As the astronauts began their training, engineers built the safest rockets ever. Yet no one knew exactly what would happen when a human blasted off; no one knew what it would be like to head into space. Like Columbus, his eyes on the horizon, wondering if the world was flat after all, all an astronaut could do was get inside this new ship and sail it across the sky.

NASA decided it wasn't ready to send a human into space. So in 1961, Ham the chimp rode in a capsule atop a rocket. It shot straight up through the sunlight and on into the darkness. It curved back to Earth, diving through the clouds into the sea. It was towed to a ship and lifted on board. Yes, the capsule had returned, but had Ham survived? Americans held their breath as the capsule door was opened. And there Ham sat, beaming and chattering to the cameras.

So space travel was possible! The United States could win the space race now, but only if it hurried.

Then in April 1961 a Soviet named Yuri Gagarin blasted into orbit. At last a human being was taking a trip through space.

Gagarin was only up there for ninety minutes, but his voyage meant the Soviets had beaten the United

Ham the chimp was four years old when he made his space flight in 1961. Scientists used banana rewards to train him.

States again. It wasn't until a month later that the first American zoomed into space. Squeezed inside a capsule smaller than a phone booth, Alan Shepard sped from zero to five thousand miles per hour in less than three minutes.

After that, more and more manned flights raced through the heavens. Both the Soviet Union and America were learning what space was like. Astronauts began to fly in teams and link up or rendezvous with other spacecraft. They took long weightless strolls in the blackness. They began to stay in space for days or weeks at a time. There were seventeen manned American missions before NASA tried shooting a rocket to the moon. The Soviets, still racing to be the first to get there, launched about as many manned spacecraft as the United States did.

Then something strange started to happen. A new kind of litter began to appear. Bag after bag of trash suddenly swam through the blackness. Humans were in space, and they were leaving their personal garbage behind. The hatch, or door, of a spacecraft would be opened by astronauts and they'd dump out almost anything they didn't need—empty food packages, old equipment, even their urine.

No one was thinking about polluting the heavens. Not a single scientist seemed worried about debris. Fortunately, this garbage was not that far from Earth. Unlike objects in higher orbit, it all burned up in the atmosphere after a few months.

The space race was proceeding at full speed;

nothing could be more exciting than reaching the moon. All eyes were nearly glued to that one shining object—and almost completely blind to the orbiting hunks of junk.

By July 1969 two manned American missions had flown close to the moon. There was only one feat left to perform, and that was to land on it. After all these years had passed, would the United States finally beat the Soviets?

People everywhere were watching and waiting as America's *Apollo 11* moon mission left on a nine-day flight. The spacecraft that blasted off was 363 feet long— longer than a football field. It weighed over six million pounds—about as much as three thousand buses. The top stage of the rocket alone had three different sections.

This mission was the most dangerous humans had ever flown. People had never before walked on ground that wasn't Earth's. Everything had to work perfectly, or the astronauts might die. A second's delay could mean they wouldn't be able to return to Earth. The tiniest mistake could mean they'd be stranded forever on the moon. They were in terrible danger, but if they succeeded, they would make history.

Then suddenly the astronauts were on the moon, laughing and jumping. Their suits had so many layers that they looked like stuffed toys. Their gloves were so thick they could hardly feel what they touched. It was 200 degrees in the sun, and −200 in the shade. There was no weather or water, so their footprints would never disappear.

Neither would the garbage they dropped on the surface—plastic and paper and other kinds of junk. They also left behind the bottom of their lunar module, the small spacecraft that flew them down to the moon's surface. When it was time to take off, the bottom part separated and was used as a launching pad.

So on the very first trip human beings took to a strange new world, we planted a flag—and left a pile of garbage.

More trash for the moon was still to come. After *Apollo 11,* there were five more lunar landings. The bottom of each lunar module stayed behind on the moon, along with three vehicles known as moon buggies. This was what some astronauts rode in when they explored the moon's surface. Astronauts deposited more and more garbage; they also abandoned $5 million worth of camera equipment. One of them even left behind two golf balls he was trying to play with. And that's not counting what the Soviets left when their unmanned craft landed on the moon.

The space race kept speeding along, with no one anxious about all the litter. In 1971 the Soviets launched the first space station. Two years later, the United States sent its own up, naming it *Skylab.* Twelve thousand instruments were on board this two-hundred-

Edwin "Buzz" Aldrin during the first moon walk. He and astronaut Neil Armstrong left assorted junk on the moon, including cameras, tools, "moonshoes," backpacks, and a bundle of garbage from their flight.

thousand-pound craft, including eight telescopes pointed at the sun.

Just like a windmill, *Skylab* had four arms. They were huge boards called solar panels, divided into squares. Each panel carried thirty thousand solar cells that turned sunlight into electricity. There was also a shield that protected *Skylab* against meteoroids and dust.

Skylab was damaged when it first went into orbit. Its shield tore off and one of its solar panels vanished.

Skylab didn't stay up very long. It slowly began to fall and in 1979 entered our planet's atmosphere. No one was sure where it would land; no one could control its descent. The biggest piece of space junk ever, it crashed in pieces to the ground.

Despite this, *Skylab* helped scientists understand how humans could spend a long time in space. One team of astronauts stayed in it for eighty-four days. It also taught experts about the sun and the Earth. It was America's only space station, but the Soviets have orbited eight. A cosmonaut lived aboard one for about eleven months. In fact, cosmonauts altogether have spent more than sixty-five hundred days in space. Americans have only spent about two thousand days there.

Everyone was getting used to people speeding through the heavens. By now the space race seemed slower, blast-offs everyday events. Manned missions, however, weren't the only flights exploring space. Satellites and probes were also streaking through the darkness.

Two-hundred-thousand-pound *Skylab*, the world's biggest piece of space junk, acted not only as a science laboratory but as a TV station, a doctor's office, and an observatory before it tumbled back to Earth.

It all started in 1960 when America launched the first communications satellite. *Echo* was just an aluminum-coated balloon that reflected radio waves back to Earth like a mirror. But by being in orbit a few hundred miles high, it began to change the way people the world over lived. Suddenly long-distance phone calls were easier to make, and television programs could be broadcast farther.

Then a new communications satellite named *Telstar* was launched. It was 1962, and the globe was made to seem even smaller. Television programs were relayed between Europe and the United States; overseas phone calls became more common.

But by 1965 even *Telstar* was out of date. Our communications satellites had become bigger and could travel farther. *Early Bird* was the first satellite to whiz to geosynchronous orbit. A satellite in such an orbit circles at just the right speed to keep it constantly over the same spot on Earth. The orbit is 22,300 miles high— one-tenth of the distance to the moon.

As the years passed, hundreds of communications satellites soared into geosynchronous orbit. Today 109 countries can watch the Olympic games live. Thirty thousand phone calls can be made overseas at once.

But think of all the multistage rockets it took to boost those satellites past the clouds.

From 1960 on, overhead traffic kept growing heavier. Both the United States and the Soviet Union launched many different kinds of satellites. Later, countries in Europe and Asia sent satellites up, too.

Some forecast weather, predicting storms and photographing the movements of clouds. They even had instruments on board that took the planet's temperature. Over the years weather satellites grew from two to fourteen feet, so that now they're powerful enough to see right through fog.

Navigational satellites helped planes and ships figure out the best routes to follow across the sky and ocean.

A 1987 weather satellite before launch to geosynchronous orbit.

Known as Navstars, they could warn of bad weather and find a ship that was sinking or a plane that had crashed. Research satellites studied everything about space, from the different kinds of radiation to a comet 44 million miles away.

Other satellites watched our planet and made very accurate maps. In eighteen days they were able to photograph every mile of the globe. Landsats, as they were called, orbited around the poles instead of the equator, helping to prove Earth was slightly pear-shaped, not round.

As time went by, satellites became more sophisticated. They stopped running on batteries and, like *Skylab*, used solar power. Some of them even made electricity from nuclear power. They could still be as small as basketballs, but now they were also as big as trucks.

Some satellites overhead could tell how strong the ocean's waves were. They had instruments on board that helped fishermen find fish. Satellites also predicted droughts and indicated when forests should be replanted.

There were even spy satellites. Equipped with powerful cameras, they could spot military tanks or ships on the move. They took perfect photographs of people from one hundred miles up. Then their film was placed in a capsule and parachuted back to Earth. An airplane flying right under it snatched the capsule in midair.

Spy satellites now are even more powerful. Some of them can orbit sixty thousand miles from Earth. Others can listen in on telephone conversations. A few have cameras on board that can spot football-sized objects from one hundred miles away.

To keep track of all satellites, special stations were built on the ground. The stations use radar to locate and follow the satellites. An instrument sends radio waves into space through an antenna. The waves bounce off a satellite the way light is reflected by a mirror, and come right back to the instrument on the ground. Tracking stations can tell how far away a satellite is at that very moment and the direction in which it is moving.

But like any kind of machine, eventually satellites wear out. If they are not solar powered, their fuel may run out. If they are solar powered, space particles can destroy their solar cells. Their computers may break or meteoroids can damage them. They may slow down enough to be pulled to Earth by gravity.

Many satellites simply keep orbiting after they die. They may circle above us for just a few months if their orbit is about two hundred miles from Earth, but a large number will stay up for hundreds of years because they're in higher orbits. In geosynchronous orbit, 22,300 miles up, satellites may orbit for more than a million years. And so many are in geosynchronous orbit at this time that sometimes they actually block each other's signals.

Over five thousand satellites have been launched by now, but for a long time no one believed the sky could become crowded. After all, didn't wide-open space yawn endlessly above us? Besides, once satellites were in use, it was hard to remember how people had lived without them. Pollution was a problem we thought we could put off solving for a while.

Probes were also racing through the darkness, lifted into space by multistage rockets. Nearly every planet has been visited at least once. Three thousand pictures were taken of Mercury despite its eight-hundred-degree heat. Twenty-one spacecraft have landed on Venus, all to be crushed by its heavy atmosphere. Robots have landed on Mars, exploring it under a pink sky. Four probes have flown past Jupiter, which is eleven times bigger than Earth. They've shown us the seventeen moons of Saturn, the black rings of blue-green Uranus, and the gigantic storm cloud of Neptune.

But probes have also left rocket stages slicing through the blackness. Like satellites, some of these probes are dead now, just wandering through space. Others continue to broadcast reports back to Earth. *Voyager II,* for example, will transmit pictures to us well into the twenty-first century.

Toward the end of the 1970s, the Solar System became an even busier highway. It was no longer just the Soviets and Americans filling the skies. The European Space Agency began to launch satellites. Its members included Belgium, Denmark, France, Germany, Italy, the Netherlands, Spain, Sweden, Switzerland, the United Kingdom, and Canada. India, China, and Japan shot off rockets, too.

Just about that time scientists began to realize orbits

might get clogged. Certain experts began to study what to do about space junk. Then in 1981 the United States produced a new kind of spacecraft, one that could go two hundred fifty miles high but leave nothing behind. It had forty-nine engines, two thousand switches, five computers, and twenty-three antennas. It was called a shuttle, and it was made in four gigantic parts. Two solid rocket boosters and an external fuel tank took the place of multistage rockets. Then there was the orbiter, where the astronauts rode. This was covered with thirty thousand tiles to protect it from heat.

The boosters parachuted into the ocean, were picked up, then used again. The external fuel tank burned up in the atmosphere. The orbiter came back to Earth, gliding in like a plane down a three-mile runway at two hundred miles per hour.

Unlike earlier spacecraft, the shuttle left no rocket stages in space. Plus, every piece of litter was stored and brought down to the ground. The only junk left above was some tiles that fell off the orbiter.

By now the shuttle has lifted off successfully some thirty times and disastrously once—the tragic launch of the *Challenger,* which exploded. But the United States launched thirty-one manned flights before developing this spacecraft that didn't litter. The Soviet Union has sent up even more manned missions. And don't forget the hundreds of probes and the thousands of satellites. That's an awful lot of garbage to scatter while traveling through space.

There's an old saying: What goes up must come

The launch of America's space shuttle *Columbia* on April 17, 1981. This shuttle was the first manned spacecraft that left no rocket stages in orbit.

down. But when a spacecraft rockets beyond Earth, it may not return for centuries. Scientists thought most of these machines would burn up in the atmosphere, but some of them just haven't slowed down enough to be dragged low by gravity. So now even after all these years, tons of useless trash are up there.

At night some of this space junk may glisten like stars. By day on the ground, we can't see it at all. To most of us it's invisible, an unseen enemy. What's up there anyway, and what exactly is it doing?

4

Trouble

Billions of years ago, an asteroid belt formed between Jupiter and Mars. So many chunks of rock, dust, and metal whirled in a thick stream that a part of space seemed to clog up. There was nothing like it anywhere else in our solar system.

But now that's about to change. Twenty years from now there may be a new kind of asteroid belt. It won't be far away—it will dance around *our* planet. Completely man-made, it will be chock full of space junk.

What took nature so long to make may only take *us* about fifty years.

Right now countless pieces of litter are circling overhead. Most of them are in orbit two hundred to seven hundred miles high (that's what scientists call low to medium Earth orbit). About seven thousand pieces are four inches in size or larger. Forty thousand are as small as a third of an inch. Nobody's really sure, but there may be one hundred billion even tinier bits.

Why worry about specks you can barely tell are there? Because a chip no bigger than your fingernail can make a spacecraft blow up. Why? It's traveling so fast it packs a gigantic punch. Remember—there's nothing in space to slow objects down. So if a flake of paint peels off a spacecraft, or a particle of dust falls outside when the hatch is opened, it will travel at the same speed as the spacecraft—many thousands of miles per hour.

Ninety-five percent of everything man-made that is now in orbit has broken down or blown up or somehow turned into junk. That's right—only 5 percent of what's up there is still working.

Of course, when the space program first started, scientists thought most orbiting objects would slow down and fall back to Earth. Five hundred to one thousand a year do exactly that: Gravity gets hold of them and they burn up in the atmosphere. But that isn't enough to reduce the crowding overhead. It's taking longer for things to fall than was first expected.

There are still nearly one thousand used-up rocket

This computer-produced long view of the Earth shows the densest band of orbiting objects, about two hundred to seven hundred miles from our planet. Although the junk two hundred miles up may only orbit for months, anything that is six hundred or more miles away will circle for centuries, while the objects that are farthest away will stay up for more than a million years.

stages spinning through space. About fourteen hundred dead satellites are circling in silence. Eighty have broken into bits while in orbit, six of them in 1987 alone. Every year we launch more rockets, more satellites, more probes; every year three hundred to five hundred more objects turn into junk.

All this garbage makes more garbage. When a rocket

stage drops off in space, it may still have fuel and oxygen left inside it. Eventually these may mix; when that happens, there's an explosion. If a rocket stage blows up, it blasts thousands of metal bits through space's vacuum. Some of them fall and burn up in Earth's atmosphere. But some of them twirl into higher and higher orbits, racing at the speed the explosion has pushed them to—a speed that's even faster than that of the rocket itself. After a while they slow down a bit and start to sink. The paths around our planet get sprinkled with circling space junk.

This has happened already. In 1986, four hundred ninety miles above the Earth, a European Space Agency rocket suddenly exploded. When the blast ripped it apart, chunks were thrown up an additional three hundred fifty miles. Other parts settled into an orbit two hundred seventy miles high. Five hundred pieces were four inches or larger. Five thousand were bits even smaller than that.

The rocket was scattered high and low over five hundred seventy miles. One piece of space junk had instantly become fifty-five hundred separate bits, making the orbiting collections of junk even bigger.

Today the same kind of rockets still orbit Earth, and there's a continuing risk that others will suddenly blow up. After seven American rocket stages had exploded by 1981, U.S. scientists redesigned them so their fuel would be completely used up. The United States is trying to get other countries to do that, too.

Yet American rockets may continue to blast apart in space. And it won't be an accident; it will be done on purpose. It's part of the testing for a military program called the Strategic Defense Initiative, nicknamed "Star Wars."

Some scientists believe space should be our planet's next battleground. They're trying to build the most powerful weapons ever and float them beyond the clouds. They hope these weapons will prevent enemies from attacking.

Their plan would work like this. Suppose nuclear bombs flew toward the United States in rockets called missiles. Special satellites would warn the authorities. Then weapons orbiting in space would destroy the missiles while they were still above the Earth. Yet another satellite would indicate whether or not all of them had been shot down. If they hadn't, missiles fired from the ground would destroy the rest of them.

In order to learn just how to do this, military scientists once made special rockets collide. From the safety of Earth, they aimed one rocket at another. The rockets blasted apart like a volcano spitting ash. Thousands of splinters of garbage spilled into space.

In 1985, a military test took place high above Earth, so all those rocket chunks stayed in orbit, increasing our space junk problem. Now the tests are being held much closer to the surface. That way the garbage will fall more quickly into the atmosphere. Within six months, the crowding overhead will be reduced.

Despite this, some experts are still concerned. By the time Star Wars is ready for launching, at some point in the next century, orbits could be crowded with all kinds of space junk. The weapons might end up being smashed by whirling pieces of trash.

But something that's even more frightening could happen. Satellites might mistake a hunk of litter for a missile. Instead of making nations safer, Star Wars might be making the world more dangerous. Instead of establishing peace on Earth, this plan might start a war in space.

As more debris floods through the heavens, it gets harder to avoid collisions. One United States satellite, nicknamed "Solar Max," was hit by two hundred pieces of speeding litter, one of which was identified as a particle of frozen urine. Solar Max was repaired by shuttle astronauts and is still functioning. In 1981 a Soviet satellite called *Cosmos 1275* shattered into almost three hundred fragments. The Soviets believe it was rammed by debris.

The more collisions there are, the greater the amount of junk. In low Earth orbit, this trash can go any which way. All those exploding pieces don't move in straight lines—they fly around madly in all directions, possibly crashing into each other and larger objects.

In the silence of space, rockets suddenly explode, and satellites are broken into pieces. But even smaller bits of litter are swimming out there, too, some of them so tiny it is nearly impossible to recognize them. There are probably billions of flecks of paint that have flaked off spacecraft, as well as pinheads of dirt or metal that have fallen from rocket stages as they separated. There are even snips of garbage that come from starting up rocket engines. To zoom forward, a spacecraft fires booster rockets; to turn, it fires retrorockets. Some of these engines use solid fuel. Solid fuel is as rubbery as a pencil eraser. It's made of oxygen, aluminum, and different chemicals. Each time these solid fuel engines fire, they spit out bits of a mineral called aluminum oxide.

All these tiny crumbs of garbage can be extremely dangerous. In 1983, as the crew lay sleeping on board the *Challenger* (the space shuttle that exploded just a few years later), a paint chip hit the window and left a pea-sized pit. Not much of a dent, you're thinking; what's so frightening about that?

But consider carefully what happened. The paint chip was very tiny—so small you could hardly have seen it. Scientists discovered it measured under one-tenth of an inch. And it weighed so little it couldn't have budged even the smallest scale. On Earth it would have landed as lightly as a dead leaf on the ground.

Yet in space conditions are different. Up there something nearly invisible can break a shuttle window. Up there something practically weightless can almost crack the window open. And if that had happened, the astronauts might have died.

Why does a paint chip have such power in space? Speed.

Remember—objects in space can travel much faster than objects on Earth. The paint chip that hit the window was traveling four miles per second. That's over fourteen thousand miles an hour—twenty-four times faster than a jet plane. On Earth we think that's racing, but in space it's just a stroll; most bits of space junk zip along even more quickly. They average twenty-two thousand miles per hour—thirteen times speedier than a bullet. Some of the teeniest pieces whiz along at thirty-four thousand miles per hour.

When something travels that fast, its punch is much greater than its size. A half-inch speck of junk has the force of a car traveling thirty miles per hour. For the shuttle to be destroyed, it wouldn't have to crash into a rocket—a quarter-inch chip can go right through its walls. A half-inch bit will hit it like a hand grenade. An astronaut on a spacewalk can be killed by a fifth-of-an-inch fleck—if it's traveling at average speed it can cut right through a spacesuit.

And don't forget the garbage in space that people have left behind. Human beings seem to be litterbugs no matter where they go. Speeding around the globe at one time or another were nuts and bolts that astronauts dropped while trying to fix spacecraft, containers that once held oxygen, and packages once filled with

While astronaut Sally Ride and the rest of the crew of the *Challenger* lay sleeping (*above right*), a speck of space junk no bigger than a grain of sand slammed into the shuttle window. It left this pea-sized crater, shown in enlargement (*below right*).

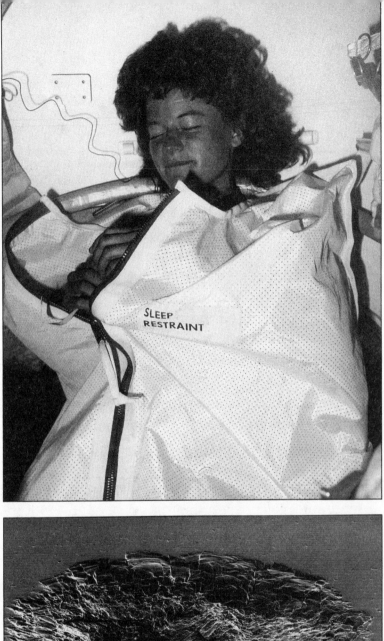

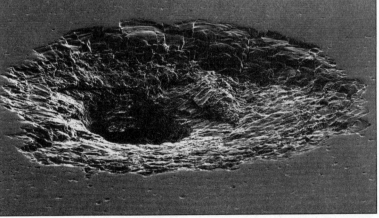

food. Swimming above our heads were used-up space-walk equipment, bags of assorted litter, even sewage that astronauts had dumped overboard. The glove that Ed White dropped on the first American spacewalk, the camera Michael Collins lost as he floated near *Gemini 10,* and the screws that slipped from George Nelson's hands as he drifted near the space shuttle all circled the Earth for months at a time. And let's not forget the garbage Soviet cosmonauts scattered around. By now, almost all this trash has burned up in the atmosphere. But it's clear that human beings working in space will continue to lose tools and belongings—just as they do on Earth.

Scientists worry that some piece of space junk will cause a serious accident soon. There's only a one-in-a-million chance now that a shuttle will hit something four inches or larger. But there's a one-in-three-thousand chance it will be damaged by a quarter-inch speck. And if space junk keeps mounting up, the chances will be one in ten by the time you have children.

It's not just the shuttle that experts are nervous about. In 1995 a new American space station may be placed in orbit, and there's a fifty-fifty chance some bit of speeding trash will damage it. The United States has spent a billion dollars to launch the Hubble Space Tele-

During his historic spacewalk in 1965, astronaut Ed White dropped a glove, which for several months became another bit of space junk orbiting the Earth. In later years astronauts dropped a camera, a toothbrush, a comb, a screwdriver, and various nuts and bolts.

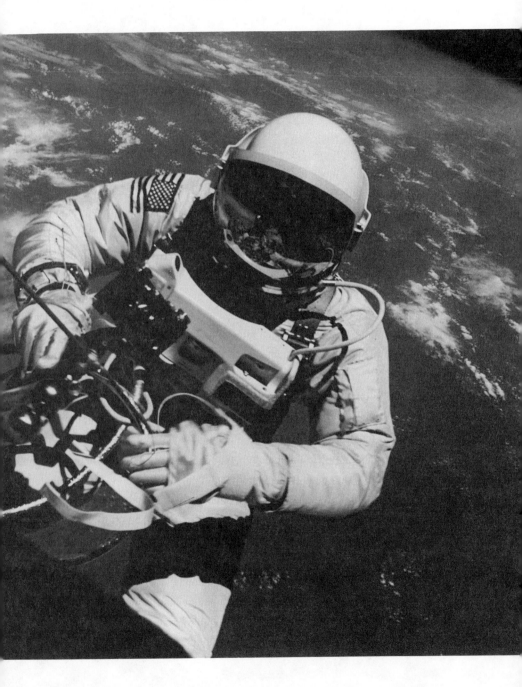

scope. The most powerful telescope in the world, it will see to the far side of the universe. There's a one-in-a-hundred chance a piece of space junk will destroy it. And there's a fifty-fifty chance some chip will seriously damage it.

The telescope might even be ruined by space junk that never touches it. That's because orbiting garbage reflects the sun. When bits of litter go roaring around our planet, they can sparkle and shine just like stars. But their light might grow too bright and eat through the telescope's sensors. Sensors are what enable the Hubble to peer so far. They were put there to search for even the dullest of gleams.

Even if the litter's glow doesn't prove too strong, the speed all those bits are racing at could wreck the telescope. In order to stay steady as it orbits, the Hubble has three trackers, each fixed on one star. What would happen if one of those "stars" was actually a piece of space junk? The telescope would try to follow it, no matter how fast it was moving. But if it couldn't stay with the trash, it would begin to spin wildly. It would shiver as if it were cold and possibly never work right again.

Here's something else to keep in mind. Out there somewhere, a piece of junk whips through space. Its

Astronomers are concerned that the billion-dollar Hubble Space Telescope, shown here as it is being prepared for space flight, may be damaged by orbiting debris.

A United States and a Canadian officer examine one of the few pieces of space junk recovered in North America.

light is a little weak, its pace a bit slow. The Hubble spots it and follows it. It doesn't know the glow is garbage. Back here on Earth scientists study what's been found. Perhaps, they say to themselves, an important discovery has been made. How can they know that what's been sighted is litter? They may think a new star has been observed.

A mistake like this isn't impossible. In fact, something like it actually happened. Canadian scientists thought a distant bright light was a strange new object giving off what are called gamma rays. The scientists believed it sat throbbing in a corner of our galaxy. But it turned out to be *Cosmos 1400,* a dead Soviet satellite. Sunlight was reflecting off its solar panels.

Gamma rays are the reason the United States is launching the new Gamma Ray Observatory. After its lift-off in 1990, this special satellite should spend years searching for radiation made by stars and galaxies. It was also built to find out what causes fierce explosions of gamma rays. These rays are invisible and wash in waves across space. Radioactive materials give off gamma rays. Scientists hope gamma rays will reveal secrets about the universe.

A chunk of garbage could wreck the Observatory as easily as you scrunch a piece of paper. And even if it isn't destroyed or damaged, it may not be able to do its job. Scientists are afraid there's a kind of space pollution that can confuse the Observatory. This pollution is caused by nuclear power.

Nuclear energy is sometimes used by spacecraft. Some blast off from Earth carrying machines called nuclear reactors. Others have on board a substance called plutonium. When plutonium breaks apart or a reactor starts working, the energy produced can be turned into electricity. This electricity powers the craft.

Many small spacecraft don't use nuclear power. They have solar cells instead, which change sunlight into electricity. But nuclear power can last longer than solar cells. It can also make a lot more electricity.

That's why it's nuclear power that sends probes roaming through the Solar System. Solar cells couldn't do this because the sun is too far away. And it's nuclear power that lets probes land and stay on Mars. Since the sun sets there at night, solar cells wouldn't be effective.

But spacecraft that run on nuclear power spit out waves of radiation. When that happens millions of miles from home, it doesn't matter to us here. After all, there has always been radiation—it was born with the universe. That's why scientists send up satellites full of instruments to study it. They feel that understanding radiation will help explain how the universe was formed.

But when spacecraft close to Earth give off radiation, satellites and observatories can't tell what to track. Just as space junk shines like stars, radiation that's manmade seems like the waves that have always raced through space.

In the last few years the best American instruments have gotten mixed up. They've tracked radiation from Soviet reactors in orbit as though it wasn't pollution. They've identified gamma rays from Soviet nuclear satellites in Earth orbit as coming from outside our solar system. Scientists fear the Gamma Ray Observatory could end up doing this, too.

As you get older, this kind of false information might become more common. The greatest space inventions might not know the true stuff from the junk. The study of astronomy may become much more difficult. Astronomers might not be able to tell what is really out there; they might not be sure of their discoveries.

But radiation can hurt more than scientific knowledge. Nuclear energy, even far away in space, can be dangerous. When something is radioactive, its radiation is so strong it can harm people back here on Earth. Even in tiny amounts radiation can eventually cause cancer. The atmosphere around our planet usually protects us from our galaxy's radiation. But what if a spacecraft using nuclear power falls back to the ground? What if a satellite run by a reactor blows up in orbit? Not all the debris will burn up far above the clouds. Some of it could actually land here next to us.

In 1978 a Soviet nuclear satellite circled the globe. *Cosmos 954* was spying on warships at sea. Suddenly it stopped working. Then the unthinkable happened. Thousands of slivers of nuclear litter whirled through the atmosphere. They landed, shooting fire, in northern Canada, near the Arctic. No one was hurt by this deadly nuclear garbage—because no one lived there—but if it had landed in a populated area, people might have gotten sick, even died.

This rain of radiation was supposed to be impossible. What happened up there, just one hundred fifty miles overhead? The Soviets believe a piece of space junk destroyed their satellite. It whooshed right into it, and the collision blew the whole thing up.

So there was almost a disaster somewhere here on Earth. And it could happen again—orbits are more filled with trash now than in 1978. *Cosmos 954* wasn't the first or the last nuclear spacecraft. The Soviets have launched at least thirty-seven nuclear satellites. Scientists are sure at least two have plunged into the Pacific Ocean. Three more may have smashed down in unknown places.

The Soviets have tried to make their nuclear satellites safe. Now if one begins to fall, rocket engines automatically fire. They boost the reactor into a higher path called a storage orbit. Reactors are spinning up there right now. They are far enough above us to circle for about six hundred years before they begin to sink. Scientists want to make sure the reactors don't drop sooner because it will take six centuries for their radioactivity to fade.

If the rocket engines don't fire, the reactor still won't crash. As it dips close to the atmosphere it will eject its core. The most dangerous part, the core is very small, and without anything to shield it, it will burn until it disappears.

But the higher orbit the reactors fly to is just six hundred miles overhead. Other satellites are circling there, too. If one of those satellites collided with a reactor, at least a million radioactive pieces would burst forth. Over time they would spill down to a lower, more crowded orbit. Many of the splinters would burn up in the atmosphere, but the larger bits would eventually drop to Earth. If they landed near a city, hundreds of people might die from cancer.

What scientists fear most nearly happened in 1988. After *Cosmos 954*, the Soviets thought they had corrected every problem. Then a nuclear satellite named *Cosmos 1900* began to tumble out of its low orbit. Nobody worried at first—the rocket engines would send the reactor to the storage orbit. But the engines failed to fire. Then the reactor didn't spit out its core. Never mind, the Soviet scientists thought, our computers on the ground can make the engines start.

The machines gave their orders, which were beamed up through space. But the satellite didn't listen. All contact had been lost. Nuclear-powered *Cosmos 1900* was out of control.

The whole world was afraid. What if the satellite came down in a fiery storm? Radioactive debris would scatter far and wide. At the last minute, a disaster was avoided. The engines started and the reactor zoomed away. But everyone felt it was just luck that no accident had occurred.

The Soviet Union keeps sending more and more re-actors into space. Now its nuclear satellites have even *more* power. Americans may have decided to keep up with the Soviets. In the past the United States tried to avoid putting nuclear spacecraft anywhere near our planet. But now some American scientists want to put one hundred reactors right near Earth. Only nuclear power, they feel, can make Star Wars possible. They're developing plans to build the world's biggest nuclear satellites. That's the best way, they think, to keep the space stations of the future working for years. They want nuclear power to supply future bases on the moon and Mars.

But other experts disagree. They say nothing nuclear should be put right above us. Radioactive pollution will turn out to be too dangerous. It puts human life at risk and can damage the environment. What if one of those giant reactors falls to Earth? It will poison whatever is around wherever it lands. That could be crops or fish, soil or the sea. Tens of thousands of people could eventually die of cancer. Space junk is increasing while more nuclear satellites are being launched. All that will do, they fear, is increase the chance of a nuclear accident.

Of course, radioactive debris isn't the only kind that falls to Earth. And you know there doesn't have to be a crash to send junk whirling to the ground. Remember *Skylab?* It just sank. It was sent to a low orbit and it stayed there for six years. Dust and dirt near the atmosphere kept bumping into it. Slowly but surely gravity increased its hold. *Skylab* sank even lower, until the atmosphere's gases rubbed against it. Soon it wasn't speeding, and Earth sucked it down.

Everyone knew it was going to crash. What they didn't know was where or when. All over the world people were frightened. What if it fell down in enormous chunks? Even if it broke into pieces, a blizzard of debris could smash down anyplace. Just imagine if it started snowing huge flakes of metal while you were walking home from school. Or if the sky blackened with litter while you were playing in the park. You couldn't

Skylab, pictured during the first of its six years orbiting the Earth. NASA expected it to stay up for nine years, at which time the shuttle could push it to a higher orbit; but the space station fell before the first shuttle was ready for launch.

do anything but wait and hope nothing hit you.

Skylab came down in a blazing shower over a desert in Western Australia. It lit up the night sky like fireworks on July 4. Once again our planet was lucky: No one was hurt. Once again that was only because hardly anyone lived where *Skylab* crashed. But five hundred pieces broke open the ground. Two of them weighed more than four thousand pounds each. Ten of them weighed more than one thousand pounds each. It was like a fleet of trucks pouring out of the clouds. Two hundred fifty pieces weighed more than ten pounds each.

Skylab's plunge was a worldwide sensation. A San Francisco newspaper had announced a prize for the first chunk of *Skylab* found. A man wandering through the desert spotted a strange lump. He got ten thousand dollars for a piece of insulation (material that protects a spacecraft from heat or cold).

Skylab is the most famous piece of space junk. It is also the biggest to drop from the sky. But it wasn't the first. What was? Nobody's sure. In 1961 a cow in Cuba was killed. What's a dead animal got to do with plunging garbage? Well, the cow was hit by something that seemed to fall from nowhere. Some people believe it was part of an American spacecraft. That same year, in Manitowoc, Wisconsin, there was a whoosh and a bang at the corner of North Eighth and Park streets. A twenty-one-pound metal fragment from *Sputnik 4* shattered the concrete in the middle of town. In 1963, a fifteen-inch metal splinter from a Russian spacecraft dropped out of the clouds. It smacked down onto a ranch in Australia. There were no cows around, but it narrowly missed a lot of sheep.

One dead cow, one smashed street, and a whole flock of terrified sheep. And that's not all.

In 1969, on the Sea of Japan, a Japanese boat was cutting through the waves. All hands on deck were watching the water. What they should have been doing was studying the sky. All of a sudden pieces of metal pelted down like hailstones. Five men were hit by wreckage from yet another Russian spacecraft.

And in 1989, space junk did it again. The sky caught fire over the middle of America. Mysterious flaming objects streaked through the night. The people who saw this were frightened. Had an invasion from Mars finally started? Were enemies bombing the United States? But the military was calm. The authorities knew what was happening: Once again a Soviet satellite had tumbled from the sky.

Space junk has landed in at least twelve countries. But more garbage by far is still orbiting Earth. Of this floating debris, approximately 45 percent is American and 47 percent is Soviet. An additional 7 percent belongs to the European Space Agency, India, China, and Japan.

Even geosynchronous orbit, so far away, is jammed. Way up there, at least there's less chance of collision because the satellites are programmed to travel in the same direction. But there's another problem with geosynchronous orbit. The satellites are keeping one another from working properly. So many are so close together that sometimes their messages to Earth are blocked.

There's a traffic jam above us that we never see. There's pollution dirtying our solar system, and we're barely aware of it. What is being done about all this space junk? Will the problem be solved before it gets beyond control?

5

Back to the Drawing Board

Close to the middle of Colorado there's a very strange mountain. It may look like the other Rockies, but don't let it fool you. Cheyenne Mountain is special. It has been hollowed out. Inside are rooms filled with eighty-seven computers. Fourteen hundred people work near them day and night. Two hundred watch the computer screens and printers all the time. What are these people doing?

Cheyenne Mountain is a part of the United States

An aerial view of Cheyenne Mountain. Here, in an underground complex, the United States Space Command tracks orbiting objects.

Space Command. The United States Space Command is in charge of watching the orbiting junk. Its experts are the ones who calculate how much litter is really up there. They make sure a fiery chunk that streaks across the sky isn't an enemy bomb but just a piece of garbage. By keeping track of where the biggest heaps of trash are, they prevent American spacecraft from colliding with them.

Twenty-six radar stations and six telescopes located around the world constantly feed the Cheyenne Mountain computers facts and pictures. Every day their screens show up to eighty thousand objects. Each computer can draw the orbit of one hunk of junk at a time. As if it were a wave, the orbit is a line curling across the screen. Each computer can also create a colored map of the world. To the person studying it, it's like a page from an atlas. Called a Mercator projection, it can be used to show where a piece of debris is traveling. A red X blips silently across the map, outlining its orbit.

Radar teaches the experts most of what they know about space junk, just the way it helps them to track satellites. Radio waves are beamed into space. When they hit a hunk of flying trash, they are reflected back

One of the several hundred crew members at Cheyenne Mountain's Space Surveillance Center follows an object in space.

This radar station in Cape Cod, Massachusetts, is used to detect missiles and to track objects in space.

to the ground. The waves show the experts how big that hunk is and exactly where it is located. They even measure the speed it is traveling around the globe. As long as the waves keep beaming overhead, they can follow the hunk as though they were bloodhounds.

Radar makes it easy to track anything tennis-ball size or larger, so the orbits of space junk four inches and up can be mapped by scientists. But radio waves cannot find fragments less than four inches in size, and lots of trash is smaller than that.

Experts divide these little bits into two different sizes. There are chips smaller than a tennis ball but as big as a marble; and there are specks that are tinier than marble size. High-powered telescopes are used to search for chips smaller than a tennis ball but as big as a marble. These chips appear as streaks of light flashing between the stars. Scientists separate the sky into a certain number of sections. They look deep into just one part and count all the streaks they see. Then they multiply that total by the number of sections. That's how they figure out how much litter surrounds our planet.

But while telescopes let scientists spot these chips, they cannot help track them. So experts don't know the exact paths any of the chips travel. And because they can't predict where the chips are going, they can't make sure spacecraft stay out of their way.

It's the tinier-than-marble-size specks that are the most mysterious. No instrument on Earth is powerful enough to find them, so these close-to-invisible bits can't even be seen. And anything unseen can't possibly be followed. All scientists can do is estimate how many there are. They have to guess the direction specks are moving in. But the experts are positive they're up there because spacecraft and satellites have come back scarred.

Most of the litter above us is so tiny it's never been tracked. In fact, millions of flecks of garbage have yet to be discovered. But the pollution is getting so thick now scientists feel that has to change. They want to be able to trace all sizes, from rockets to flakes of paint. Otherwise spacecraft will keep soaring into danger. Scientists have to know where the junk is in order to help spacecraft avoid it.

Right now, NASA is trying to invent much better ways of tracking. It hopes to orbit a special satellite with a powerful telescope on board. This telescope will be able to see waste that is tinier than raindrops. NASA also plans to develop a brand-new radar system. With it, radio waves will find and follow bits the size of M&Ms.

But even with better instruments telling more and more about space junk, experts still won't be able to prevent crashes between the smallest of slivers and spacecraft. Objects as huge as the shuttle or the future American space station can't move quickly or easily enough to dodge them and dart away. The only way to protect these huge craft is to put very strong shields on them.

The space station will be bigger than any other craft ever launched—508 feet long. If the Washington Monument were lying on its side, it would be only a little longer. The station will be so big and heavy that no

This is a drawing of the planned space station in which astronauts from the United States, Japan, and the European Space Agency will live for six months at a time. A shield is being built to protect it from space junk.

rocket yet built is powerful enough to lift it. So the shuttle will be used to fly it up in separate parts. It will take at least five flights to get all the pieces into the heavens. Astronauts will put it together as if it were an Erector Set. Because it's so large and will orbit for years, it will get nicked by more junk more often than anything before it.

To protect the space station, engineers are building a special covering called an aluminum bumper shield. This ten-thousand-pound shield will have two layers. The outer layer is the one that will get smacked by speeding trash, but it will be strong enough to shatter anything but huge pieces. The inner layer will act more like a pillow, preventing the blow the outer layer receives from denting the station. Sections of this bumper shield are already in place around the most important parts—the rooms on board where the astronauts will work and live.

But no shield can protect the station from the largest chunks of junk. There's only one way to prevent a disaster, and that's to make sure the station and the junk don't collide. NASA wants to develop a faster and more exact warning system than the one at Cheyenne Mountain. The new system would spot dangerous trash so far away it would be hours before the trash arrived at the space station. Even a huge space station could escape if it had that much notice.

Some experts think the best lookout would be a special satellite orbiting near the station. Like a watchdog outside a house, it would guard the space station from oncoming litter. Other scientists think it might be better to have radar or a telescope on board the station. Whenever a menacing object was discovered, an alarm would instantly sound. That would signal the crew to fire the station's small jets in order to maneuver out of the way. Trackers on the ground would also radio the astronauts in case they missed the first warning.

With the bumper shield guarding against the smaller bits of garbage and alarms warning the crew about the gigantic ones nearby, the space station would have a better chance to circle our planet with the astronauts free from risk. It should be able to stay safely in orbit for many years more than *Skylab* did.

But right now most of our spacecraft fly through the heavens unprotected. The Hubble Space Telescope doesn't even have a thin shield. The Gamma Ray Observatory just has some covering for its sensors. Neither can dash away if a gob of garbage soars near. All scientists can do to help them is guard their instruments from unwanted radiation. Their computers have been reprogrammed to do this, but no one is really sure it will work.

The space shuttle is also in danger. Some experts worry each time it blasts off. Will this be the mission that has an accident caused by litter? At this point the best way to protect the shuttle is to plan its orbit very carefully. That way it will avoid the paths of the largest pieces of junk. And if anything big does zip close, trackers on Earth can warn the astronauts, who will quickly fire the shuttle's rockets and glide to safety.

Scientists have realized for a while that they do not know enough about space junk. In the past few years experts in the United States have been trying to learn more. NASA has what it calls the Space Debris Assessment Program Plan. The people who are part of it study how pollution above us can be controlled. They are trying to figure out all the ways littering can be stopped. They're working on methods to bring what's already above us back down.

In 1988 the White House also grew concerned about floating garbage. The highest government officials realized junk was threatening the U.S. space program. They knew NASA was making changes in the way astronauts travel through the heavens, but what about the other countries blasting rockets off the ground? The wastebasket past the clouds could be filled up by them even if America completely stopped littering. So a group within the White House was formed to talk to other countries. They, too, had to recognize that space junk was a problem. Today the European Space Agency has what it calls an orbital debris group. And Japan is trying to be more careful about what its rockets leave behind.

Right now experts are working on a variety of methods that one day might reduce the heaps of trash in space. NASA wants to use paint that won't flake off spacecraft, but no one's been able to develop any yet. It also wants to design a new kind of rocket so no more splotches of dirt spit out when stages separate. If NASA has its way, this new rocket would also use a new fuel. Much cleaner than the old type, it won't spray dirt out

On *Skylab*, shown here, bags of trash were stored rather than dumped. But the Soviet space station *Mir* still sends its trash into space.

the nozzles when the rocket engines are fired. But engineers might need years to build this better machine; in the meantime they have to use the kind they know pollutes the blackness.

Even today, after years of studying pollution, no one is quite sure how to clean up the mess above us. NASA once thought its plan to have dead rockets burn up all their fuel meant those useless ghosts would no longer be a danger. But although there's no risk of explosion, there's still the possibility of a crash as long as the rockets up there are circling Earth. Some scientists now say they have a better idea, one that gets these floating tombs completely out of the way. All rocket stages would be programmed to restart in space. They would fly down close to Earth to what is called a disposal orbit. There they would sink into the atmosphere and burn to ashes, or fall from the sky and splash down in the ocean.

NASA is experimenting with all sorts of new ideas. It's trying to develop a new type of satellite, one that would mean fewer useless hulks in space. This one would have on board a duplicate of every important part. If one part went dead or was damaged by speeding garbage, the backup part could easily take over.

Experts are trying to program computers to see into the future. They want to create what's called a model of space junk patterns. The computer will be told how litter flies through the blackness, what happens during crashes, and where fragments usually end up. NASA hopes this information will someday help computers predict all the places near our planet where pollution will spread.

But not every idea has to wait until tomorrow. Scientists are doing something now that helps stop the piles of junk from getting bigger. NASA has figured out a way to put some satellites in orbit without using extra rockets to lift them off the ground. And once those satellites break down or are damaged by space junk, they no longer just circle our planet for years.

How did NASA do this? It's part of the reason why the shuttle was built. The shuttle is big enough to carry satellites into space. It has done this many times already, opening its huge cargo doors so a satellite can fire its own small engines and roar into orbit.

Sometime in the future NASA plans to launch all of America's satellites from the shuttle. The craft will carry two kinds of rockets that can lift satellites into any orbit. After each mission, these rockets will return to the shuttle, which will be able to use them over and over again. The OMV (orbital maneuvering vehicle) will shoot a satellite far above the shuttle, while the OTV (orbital transfer vehicle) will blast it all the way to geosynchronous orbit. No junk will be left behind on any of these flights. If the satellites break down, the rockets can fetch them back for repair.

Some of the shuttle's astronauts have also been trained to fix broken satellites. When one breaks down, the orbiter is flown right up to it. Crew members float

Using the shuttle to launch satellites is one way to cut down on space pollution. Here the shuttle *Discovery* begins putting a communications satellite into orbit.

outside in what's called a service spacewalk. They try to repair the satellite; if they can't, the shuttle brings it back to Earth.

No matter how careful everyone is in space now, there will be junk spinning around our planet, weaving in between spacecraft, for many years to come. And the more time passes, the more junk will whirl above us, as crashes and collisions add pieces of debris. But sometime in the future, experts might be able to actually clean up parts of the heavens. Scientists are working on new methods now. A lot of them seem to come right out of science fiction.

Imagine that some of them have come true and you're taking a trip through space. You're zooming through the blackness on the lookout for trash when suddenly, right above you, a high net cuts through the gloom. You think, this isn't the ocean, there are no fishermen up here. But then you realize the net is for catching space junk. No salmon, or trout, or tuna swim into it— just gobs of garbage and pinpoints of dust. If the net doesn't trap them, at least it slows them down. And the slower they move, the faster they fall to Earth.

You speed on a little farther until you see flashing rays of light beneath you. They crisscross in the darkness like lightning bolts. The glare makes you squint, but there's not a sound to be heard. You're seeing lasers and particle beams firing—some of the Star Wars weapons. They're shooting down chunks of space junk in low Earth orbit as if a war were being fought. With their enormous power they smash and shatter debris.

Instead of gigantic hunks slowly sinking toward our planet, now there are specks falling rapidly, and burning up in the atmosphere.

As you race along, you spot a machine that seems to be heading toward you as it eats into the darkness. You steer your craft away from it—and just in time! It's a galactic vacuum cleaner, out here in space sucking up debris. For a minute you keep worrying: Will it gobble you up, too? Then you realize there's nothing to be afraid of—it's only after space junk. Every now and then its huge dirtbag gets emptied. The filth inside is returned to Earth or flown to deep space.

Now you're set to rocket to the moon, but before you leave low Earth orbit, you spot the shuttle just below you, with astronauts floating outside. It moves forward a little, then stops, then starts again. It seems to be making pickups, with the crew following beside. Once in a while the astronauts scoot over and grab an object. Then they zip over to the shuttle and shove it through the door. Suddenly you realize exactly what's going on. This is no ordinary shuttle, this is no regular crew. It's the space sanitation team from the shuttle garbage truck. They're up here above the clouds collecting the trash.

You shoot toward the moon, cutting through geosynchronous orbit. Thousands of miles from home, you find yourself in a silent graveyard. It is the junkyard orbit, where dead spacecraft stay forever. Light gleams off them, and they look like coffins. Here they are far enough away from our planet not to interfere with regular space travel.

More time passes until at last you reach the moon. It's not lifeless and empty—spacecraft after spacecraft is landing. Astronauts toss out garbage bags and leave them on the surface. The moon has become the first official trash bin of the solar system.

No one can know today how the people of the future will deal with space junk. Some of these things may happen; none of them may come to pass. Right now people are beginning to understand that space is being polluted. What you've just seen on your imaginary trip are some of the solutions from the experts' drawing boards.

But are the steps currently being taken enough to control the problem? The endless black frontier above us may be a place people can ruin. The question some scientists ask themselves is, Did we find out in time?

6

Who Owns Space?

Most people take the sky and the stars and the moon for granted. Ask them who owns space and you're likely to hear one of two answers—nobody, or everybody.

Is the question worth asking? For many centuries it really didn't matter at all whether space belonged to anyone. Nothing man-made was being sent up there. But today, as more and more rockets go even deeper through our solar system and as the junk they leave behind gets thicker around our planet, the people of Earth will to have to decide what the answer is.

Picture the future if space is settled the same way the globe was. Astronauts would race each other across the heavens as explorers once crossed the seas. Chunks of the darkness would be divided between countries. Planets would go on sale; asteroids would be for rent. Whoever got to a star first would simply grab it and keep it. When people moved in, factories would be built. There'd be traffic jams overhead, with pollution starting, then getting worse. People might end up creating problems no one can even imagine now.

While these ideas may seem farfetched, they're not completely impossible. Already many schemes are planned for space. Because the sky seems as wide open to us as the Earth did to Columbus, some people feel they can do anything up there. A few proposals are just silly; others could be dangerous. But any of them would clutter up orbits and create even more junk.

Several companies in the United States have proposed a new kind of cemetery. Instead of burying people in the ground, they would cremate their bodies and rocket their ashes into orbit. Enclosed in gleaming space coffins, they would circle above us for all time.

Some people see the sky as a gigantic billboard. They want to launch the brightest artificial lights ever to form the first space advertisements. One day you might see McDonald's golden arches spinning overhead!

Others want to create space art by lifting glowing objects past the clouds. They believe all of us on the ground should have something to look at besides the stars. American artists talk about blasting off a sparkling satellite named ARSAT. In France some people actually wanted to send up a giant piece of art called the *Ring of Light*. But astronomers from all over the world protested. They said these kinds of objects could reflect light and shine brighter than the moon. Such a strong glow would outshine real stars. The stars that didn't become invisible would be harder to spot. Astronomers feared it would be more difficult to learn about the universe.

Some countries and corporations would like space to become big business. They plan to use it to make more products and more money for themselves. They may strip-mine the moon and Mars to find new supplies of minerals. They may build all kinds of orbiting factories near Earth. And some scientists fear that as the factories spit out dirt and smoke, the sky could lose its color. It might turn mustard yellow or brown and never gleam

A drawing of a proposed mining town on the moon. The mines and living quarters are on the right. In the center is a small spacecraft.

blue again. The stars would keep on shining, but it would be impossible to see them. Space would be so filthy, it would easily block out their light.

There are also schemes to get rid of the pollution with which our planet has been soiled. Some people want to pack up our planet's garbage and shoot it through the Solar System. Others want to put toxic and radioactive waste up there, too. It doesn't matter where it goes, they say, as long as it's not near us.

You already know about the experts who want to use space to defend their countries. To them the most important reason to reach the heavens is to learn how to put it to military use. Right now 75 percent of all American spacecraft ever launched belong to some branch of the military. If Star Wars weapons get off the ground, thousands of armed satellites will be orbiting all the time.

None of this has happened yet—but who knows about the future? Now more and more countries are learning how to blast off rockets. Even private corporations are sending satellites into orbit. It's possible that one day millionaires will have their own private spaceships, just as today they own airplanes and yachts.

But if the sky has been filled with junk by just a handful of nations, what's going to happen when the whole world can travel up there? What will space be like when companies and individuals are allowed beyond the clouds?

The United States is making plans to deal with all the garbage, but there's no way to make sure all countries follow American rules. In the United States, companies must apply to the Department of Transportation for permission to launch a rocket, but there's no guarantee that will happen worldwide. Although international treaties have designed laws for space, no galactic police force is up there to enforce them. The only way the laws can work is if every nation agrees to accept them. So the sole protection for the dark frontier is the honor system.

The sky is nearly undefended, just as our planet is. Earthlings may yet do to space what they've done to the globe. Many years ago, people didn't know much about pollution. The ocean was getting dirty, but they didn't think it would be a problem. They kept dumping garbage in it; factories kept spilling their chemical wastes. After all, they told themselves, the sea is deep and wide. And when they looked at the water, the filth was hard to spot.

At the same time, the air was losing its freshness. No one got nervous—wasn't there even more air than water? Cars spat out black fumes and smelled up the streets. But no one wanted to give them up and go back to horses. How could anyone return to a time when a trip of just a few miles could take a whole day? Besides, the air was still easy to breathe. It didn't seem unhealthy.

But then the ocean grew so grimy that sometimes it was dangerous to swim in it. The rivers became so slimy that a lot of fish were poisoned and died. The air turned so gritty it wasn't always safe to leave the house. Even the atmosphere, the weather, and Earth's temperature began to change.

When the space program began, no one expected trash to be a major problem. People were so excited about this new adventure that the many warning signs were ignored. For one thing, they didn't consider that the voyages through the heavens were in just a small part of it. Most people thought when rockets blasted into space, they were soaring huge distances. But the first satellites flew only one hundred miles above the surface of the Earth. On the ground that's not much farther than Philadelphia to New York. The world's largest trash heap began pretty close to home. And garbage is still being dumped nearby today. Yet although we can't see this floating junkyard, it's sending us a message: If we don't do something about space junk soon, our problems on Earth could be repeated in space.

The time is fast approaching when everyone will have to answer two questions: What objects really need to be launched? What are the best reasons to travel to the stars? We need to think *now* about how our exploration of the heavens will affect it years into the future. Space junk is a warning; it's telling us we must be more careful of the dark frontier than we were of the ground.

So—who really does own space?

No matter where you stand on Earth, when you look up you see the sky. It doesn't matter who you are— it's there for all of us to watch. It's full of secrets and beauty, and it will be there billions of years after we've gone. It doesn't belong to any of us; we belong to it.

Bibliography

Books

Barrett, N. S. *Satellites*. New York: Franklin Watts, 1985.

Bendick, Jeanne. *Artificial Satellites*. New York: Franklin Watts, 1982.

Boorstin, Daniel J. *The Discoverers: A History of Man's Search to Know His World and Himself*. New York: Random House, 1985.

Bova, Ben. *Workshops in Space*. New York: Dutton, 1974.

Branley, Franklin M. *From Sputnik to Space Shuttles: Into the New Space Age*. New York: Crowell, 1986.

Collins, Michael. *Liftoff*. New York: Grove, 1988.

Ferris, Timothy. *Coming of Age in the Milky Way*. New York: Morrow, 1988.

Furniss, Tim. *Our Future in Space*. New York: Bookwright, 1985.

Hargrove, Eugene C., ed. *Beyond Spaceship Earth: Environmental Ethics and the Solar System*. San Francisco: Sierra Club, 1987.

Herda, D. J. *Research Satellites*. New York: Franklin Watts, 1987.

Irvine, Mat. *Satellites and Computers*. New York: Franklin Watts, 1984.

BIBLIOGRAPHY

Kerrod, Robin. *Living in Space.* New York: Crescent, 1986.

Lauber, Patricia K. *Big Dreams and Small Rockets.* New York: Crowell, 1965.

Moche, Dinah. *Astronomy Today: Planets, Stars, Space Exploration.* New York: Random House, 1982.

Ride, Sally, with Susan Okie. *To Space and Back.* New York: Lothrop, Lee and Shepard, 1986.

Wright, Pearce. *The Space Race.* New York and Toronto: Gloucester, 1987.

Articles

Broad, William J. "Orbiting Debris Threatens Space Missions." *The New York Times,* 4 August 1987, Section III, 1:5.

———. "New Plans for Space Reactors Raise Fears of Nuclear Debris." *The New York Times,* 18 October 1988, Section III, 1:5.

———. "Space Pollution Forces NASA to Change Plans for Key Projects." *The New York Times,* 27 December 1988, Section III, 1:1.

———. "The Military Has a Fleet of Satellites in Line for Takeoff." *The New York Times,* 1 January 1989, Section IV, 6:1.

———. "Russians Disclose Putting New Reactors in Space." *The New York Times,* 15 January 1989, Section I, 1:3.

———. "A Debate Over Putting Nuclear Power in Orbit." *The New York Times,* 22 January 1989, Section IV, 7:4.

Chaikin, A. "The Space Shuttle's Uncertain Environment." *Sky and Telescope,* December 1982, 527–29.

BIBLIOGRAPHY

"Close Encounters in Space." *Sky and Telescope*, June 1982, 570.

Covault, C. "SDI Delta Intercept Yields Data on Space Collision Shock Waves." *Aviation Week and Space Technology*, 8 June 1987, 26–27.

"Debris Danger Zone." *Natural History*, November 1987, 6.

Foley, T. M. "NASA Halts Design of Shielding for Satellite Nuclear Power Sources." *Aviation Week and Space Technology*, 15 December 1986, 19–20.

Frederick, D. J. "Litter in Space Increasing." *Space World*, March 1985, 17–18.

"The Great Big Garbage Dump in the Sky." *Discover*, January 1986, 15.

"Hubble Trouble?" *Sky and Telescope*, January 1987, 31.

Johnson, N. L., and D. S. McKnight. "Space Debris." *Space World*, June 1988, 7–11.

Kessler, Donald. "Junk in Space." *Natural History*, March 1982, 12 + .

———. "Space Debris." *Sky and Telescope*, June 1987, 587.

Kolcum, E. H. "Shuttle Payloads to Be Protected on Pad." *Aviation Week and Space Technology*, 28 March 1983, 16–17.

Lovece, J. A. "Impending Crisis of Space Debris." *Astronomy*, August 1987, 6–13.

Maran, S. P. "Much Ado About Flashing Points of Light." *Natural History*, September 1988, 82–84.

Marshall, E. "Space Junk Grows with Weapons Tests." *Science*, 25 October 1985, 424–25.

BIBLIOGRAPHY

Murphy, J. "Dodging Celestial Garbage." *Time*, 21 May 1984, 92.

"NASA Strategy Aimed at Cutting Risk of Orbital Collisions." *Aviation Week and Space Technology*, 5 September 1988, 217.

"Nuclear Debris Could Be Released in Shuttle/Centaur Explosion." *Aviation Week and Space Technology*, 10 March 1986, 288.

"Radioactive Space Debris Study Cites Hazards to Satellites, Earth." *Aviation Week and Space Technology*, 22 September 1986, 19–20.

"Shuttle Appears to Be a Clean Bird." *Space World*, March 1982, 26+.

"Space Shuttle Still Looking Clean." *Space World*, August 1982, 27.

"Station Likely to Be Hit by Debris." *Aviation Week and Space Technology*, 17 September 1984, 16.

"Trash in Orbit." *US News and World Report*, 19 April 1982, 96.

"Trashing Space." *Scientific American*, August 1987, 14+.

Treen, J. "Nuclear Crash?" *The Nation*, 3 October 1988, 261.

"Used Ariane Stage Explodes, Creating Space Debris Hazard." *Aviation Week and Space Technology*, 1 December 1986, 34.

Van den Bergh, S. "Century 21." *Sky and Telescope*, July 1987, 4.

Index